BRITAIN
AT WAR

RICHARD EURICH. *The Withdrawal from Dunkerque. 1940.*

This painting of the most celebrated event of this war shows troops being ferried from the beaches to the drifter and the sidewheel naval tug in the right foreground. At the far right a destroyer is departing. At the extreme left motor trucks have been lined up to form a small subsidiary pier. Across the center may be seen the jetty from which many troops were rescued.

Eurich was born in 1903 at Bradford. He studied art at the Bradford Art School and at the Slade School. An amateur yachtsman, he has specialized in naval subjects.   (Oil on canvas, 30⅛ x 40 inches)

BRITAIN AT WAR

EDITED BY MONROE WHEELER. TEXT BY T. S. ELIOT,
HERBERT READ, E. J. CARTER AND CARLOS DYER

THE MUSEUM OF MODERN ART, NEW YORK

ACKNOWLEDGMENTS

The President and Trustees of the Museum of Modern Art wish to record their deep appreciation of the services of Sir Kenneth Clark, Director of the National Gallery, London, who has been in charge of arrangements in England for the exhibition upon which this volume is based. Grateful acknowledgment is also extended to T. S. Eliot for contributing his poem, *Defense of the Islands,* to E. J. Carter and Herbert Read for their articles, and to the following persons and institutions who have generously collaborated in preparing the exhibition and book:

For Loans to the Exhibition: Acme Newspapers, Incorporated; Associated Press; L. Berman; Bill Brandt; British Library of Information, New York; British Official Photographers; Bundles for Britain, Incorporated; Mr. and Mrs. John Carter; Central Press Photos, Limited, in arrangement with British Combine Photos of New York; Stephen C. Clark; Fox Photos, Limited; *Flight;* Alexander Gross; International News Photos; Victor Levy; London *Daily Sketch;* London News Agency Photos, Limited; London *Times;* Ministry of Information, London; The National Gallery of Canada, Ottawa; *Punch;* Peter Ray; James A. Sinclair of London; Richard N. Stone; Miss Jessica Stonor; Topical Press Agency, Limited.

For Information and Counsel: David M. Bailey; E. M. O'R. Dickey; Alan A. Dudley; H. S. Ede; Sir Angus Fletcher; Talbot Hamlin; Jan Juta; E. McKnight Kauffer; H. O. McCurry, Director of The National Gallery of Canada; Lieutenant I. T. Morgan; General H. S. Sewell; Mrs. Ala Story; Lieutenant L. S. B. Worrall; Gary Underhill.

For the Camouflage Section: The camouflage section has been prepared by Carlos Dyer, of the Museum staff, with the collaboration of Stanley William Hayter, Richard Bennett, Lt. Colonel Homer Saint-Gaudens and Captain Paul W. Thompson. The models and diagrams for the camouflage section have been made by the faculty and students of The Art School of Pratt Institute, Brooklyn, New York: James C. Boudreau, Director; Alexander J. Kostellow, Supervisor of Design and Structure; William L. Longyear, Supervisor of Advertising Design; Konrad Wittmann, Chief of Industrial Camouflage Program; Major Peter Rodyenko, Chief of Military Camouflage Program; James R. Patterson, Supervisor of Exhibits; Donald R. Dohner, Supervisor of Industrial Design; Robert Kolli, Design Instructor; Ivan Rigby, Design Instructor.

For Photographs: All photographs, with the exception of those by Miss Lee Miller, have been provided by the Ministry of Information, London, and were selected by C. H. Gibbs-Smith, Misha Black, Miss Mona Beardsley and Milner Gray. The photographs by Miss Lee Miller (pages 58, 68 and 73) have been reproduced through the courtesy of Charles Scribner's Sons, New York, publishers of *Bloody But Unbowed: Pictures of Britain Under Fire.*

For Films: The films shown in connection with the exhibition were acquired by the Museum of Modern Art Film Library from the British Library of Information, New York.

For Assistance in the Preparation of the Book: Miss Lenore H. Browning, Miss Betty Chamberlain, Miss Lee Francis and Mrs. C. S. Hartman of the Museum staff.

CONTENTS

DEFENSE OF THE ISLANDS

Let these memorials of built stone—music's
enduring instrument, of many centuries of
patient cultivation of the earth, of English
verse

be joined with the memory of this defense of
the islands

and the memory of those appointed to the grey
ships—battleship, merchantman, trawler—
contributing their share to the ages' pavement
of British bone on the sea floor

and of those who, in man's newest form of gamble
with death, fight the power of darkness in air
and fire

and of those who have followed their forebears
to Flanders and France, those undefeated in de-
feat, unalterable in triumph, changing nothing
of their ancestors' ways but the weapons

and those again for whom the paths of glory are
the lanes and the streets of Britain:

to say, to the past and the future generations
of our kin and of our speech, that we took up
our positions, in obedience to instructions.

T. S. ELIOT
9. vi. 40

THE ARTIST AND NATIONAL DEFENSE

With admirable wisdom, in this war as in the last, the British Government has recognized the usefulness of art to enliven the idealism with which its people are united in self-defense, to ennoble the scene of their common suffering and to provide visual imagery of their great cause and their peril. This book and the exhibition which is its subject matter offer a necessarily limited survey of what the artist can do in time of war.

During such a war as this, the security of every nation—even a nation at peace—must be sustained with clarity and vitality of the civilian mind as well as by force of armament. Therefore the role of the creative artist in the national emergency is a decisive as well as a complex problem. The example of Great Britain in using its artists' talents in painting, drawing, cartoon, poster and camouflage may help us to find our own solutions.

1914–18; 1939–41

It was not until 1917 that the Ministry of Information made arrangements for the employment of artists to record the last war—notably Kennington, Nevinson, Wyndham Lewis, the two Nashes and the two Spencers—some of whom had already seen service and been invalided home. There was general satisfaction with their work, and just before the end of the war, or immediately after it, John, Orpen, Bone, Lavery and others were commissioned to complete the pictorial history with official portraits and retrospective paintings. In this way the collection in the Imperial War Museum was built up.

Meanwhile the Canadian Government also assembled a fine group of war pictures, a selection of which has kindly been sent to us through the courtesy of H. O. McCurry and the National Gallery of Canada, Ottawa.

Within two months of the declaration of the pres-ent war, a committee was formed under the chairmanship of Sir Kenneth Clark, Director of the National Gallery, to draw up a list of artists qualified to record the war at home and abroad, and to advise government departments on the selection of artists from this list and on such questions as copyright, disposal and exhibition of work and the publication of reproductions.

The committee consists of distinguished men professionally concerned with art, and representatives of the Admiralty, War Office, Air Ministry, Ministry of Home Security, Ministry of Supply and Ministry of Information.

Artists are employed in two categories: salaried appointments for full-time work with one or another

AUGUSTUS JOHN. A Canadian Soldier, 1917. Oil on canvas, 32 x 24 inches. Lent by the National Gallery of Canada, Ottawa.

branch of the armed forces; or particular commission and purchase.

Recalling that many of the best pictures painted of the last war were by men who saw active service, the committee has arranged that painters already in the armed forces should have opportunity to do some work of art.

With the exception of the paintings from Canada and a few additional watercolors, all the paintings in the present exhibition have been selected in London by Sir Kenneth Clark.

It is worthy of note how little false optimism, exaggerated pathos or war-time hatred these pictures show. There are three main divisions of subject matter: portraiture and the common people at all their tasks; destruction by and of the enemy; and the awe-inspiring martial machinery of defense.

There is little or no trace of corruption of the artists' taste or integrity. Indeed, in certain instances

of the abstract school—Graham Sutherland, John Piper, Henry Moore—the tragedy of war and the beauty of its mechanism seem as appropriate and personal as anything they have undertaken to paint before.

The honor the British have done their artists in summoning them to a particular role in the national defense may provide for us an object-lesson at a time when our own government is beginning the various enrollment of its citizens. No one pretends any more that international political issues and armed conflict are none of the artist's business. Like another man, he may be required to fight, and if his country loses, he may lose all that makes art possible. It would be tragic neglect, on the other hand, for anyone to be indifferent to the arts and the fate of artists in these times.

In defending a civilization there should be as little dislocation or abandonment of the civilizing arts as possible, and as much continuance and preservation as we can possibly afford. The artist is an extreme specialist and sometimes, even with the best will in the world, cannot become a first-rate soldier. The necessity of his talent for such things as posters and camouflage is well understood. And the influence of painting as a fine art may also be enlisted in the common cause, as the British have shown us. We must admire their perspicacity and courage, in spite of a shortage of man-power, in keeping so many British artists at the work they do best.

Those whose work is shown here have fought well without guns.

MONROE WHEELER

SIR WILLIAM ORPEN. Major-General Sir D. Watson, K.C.B., C.M.G., 1918. Oil on canvas, 36 x 30⅛ inches. Lent by the National Gallery of Canada, Ottawa.

THE ARTIST AND NATIONAL DEFENSE

THE WAR AS SEEN BY BRITISH ARTISTS

American visitors to London must often have found their way to the Imperial War Museum where they would find, perhaps to their surprise, one of the most interesting collections of contemporary British painting to be seen in the city. This was the result of a rather haphazard policy carried out during the last war. Encouraged by the success of this experiment, the newly formed Ministry of Information lost no time at the beginning of this war in enlisting artists in a scheme of similar scope. Leading painters and draughtsmen were appointed as official artists to the Navy, the Army and the Air Force. These artists wear uniforms, and live and work with the various units to which they are attached. They may, indeed, go into action with those units and see the worst—and the best—of the war with their own eyes. Other artists are commissioned to do special jobs on the civilian front—in the armament factories or the air-raid shelters; and any artist may submit work to a committee of the Ministry of Information who will purchase it for the nation if it is considered of sufficient interest. Already, after little more than a year of the war, a very impressive collection of war pictures has been built up, and the exhibition of these pictures at the National Gallery has attracted crowds of people. In fact the National Gallery, with this exhibition of pictures and its mid-day concerts of classical music, has become a defiant outpost of culture, right in the midst of the bombed and shattered metropolis.

It is a representative selection of these pictures which is now being exhibited in the Museum of Modern Art in New York. It includes the work of veterans like Sir Muirhead Bone and Sir William Rothenstein whose names will already be familiar in the United States; it includes the work of artists like Paul Nash and Eric Kennington who first made their reputation with their paintings of the last war; and it includes the work of several artists whose names

will be unfamiliar because it is only now, in this war, that they are revealing their exceptional talent. All these artists have had one aim: to bring us a little closer to the reality—to the pathos, the humour and the tragedy of the war—aspects of the war which only the sensitive artist can see and record. This is best done by the rapid sketch, and in the drawings of Edward Ardizzone, Anthony Gross and Feliks Topolski you will find a keen and human observation quite beyond the means of the camera. Ardizzone was with the expeditionary force in France, and his drawings give a vivid impression of that confused phase of the war. He has now been transferred to the London front, and sketches like "Shelter Scene" and "A Pub in Silvertown" convey with the fidelity and realism of a Daumier the atmosphere in which the people of London are now living. Topolski is attached to the Polish forces in Great Britain, and he shows how a true artist can snatch beauty from

SIR WILLIAM ORPEN. Man Thinking on the Butte de Warlencourt. Lent by Stephen C. Clark.

the most trivial incidents. Particular interest attaches to the vivid sketches of Midshipman Worsley, for in this case it is not an officially appointed artist who is recording an aspect of the war, but a member of the fighting forces.

All these artists, and others whose names have not been mentioned, are engaged on what might be called "reportage." To represent the reality of some aspect of the war remains their chief object, and the work of art begins and ends within this sphere of reality. But other artists begin from the reality which is the war and try to achieve a new order of reality or vision. This has been successfully achieved in Graham Sutherland's picture of air-raid damage, but one may feel that Eric Ravilious, though he has painted pictures which are as esthetically satisfying as any in the exhibition, has not told us anything of particular value about the war. The transformation of reality begins already in paintings still so obviously realistic as the portraits of Eric Kennington; his "Leading Stoker Cloke" and his "Able Seaman Povey" are no longer individuals, but representative types, figures visualized from some immense epic of war. In his portrait of "Group Captain Sweeney" you have not merely the features of a famous American hero, but the very symbol of visionary enterprise. But it is not merely the personnel of war, but the actual scene that can thus transcend reality. I am referring particularly to Paul Nash's pictures of aircraft. Here the machine which is most typical of the war is animated, is made into a monstrous bird threatening humanity from the skies. Nothing could be more desolate than these same monsters when they lie broken and defeated at the foot of some cliff or in the shallow water of the Channel: symbols of the triumph of man's free spirit over the instruments of tyranny and aggression.

It is not for an Englishman to praise these pictures for the spirit they represent, but one final word of explanation. It may be that the general effect will strike the American visitor as tame or subdued, as too quiet and harmonious for the adequate repre-

sentation of war. It must then be remembered that though the English are energetic in action, they are restrained in expression. Our typical poetry is lyrical, not epical or even tragic. Our typical music is the madrigal and the song, not the opera and the symphony. Our typical painting is the landscape. In all these respects war cannot change us; and we are fighting this war precisely because in these respects we refuse to be changed. Our art is the exact expression of our conception of liberty: the free and unforced reflection of all the variety and eccentricity of the individual human being.

HERBERT READ

EDWARD WADSWORTH. *Dazzle Ships in Drydock at Liverpool. c. 1918. Oil on canvas, 120 x 96 inches. Lent by the National Gallery of Canada, Ottawa.*

PAINTINGS: LAST WAR

ERIC KENNINGTON. *The Conquerors. 1920. Oil on canvas, 117 x 96 inches. Lent by the National Gallery of Canada, Ottawa. For biographical note on the artist see page 26.*

Men of the 16th Canadian Scottish Battalion, First Division, marching from Arras to Amiens.

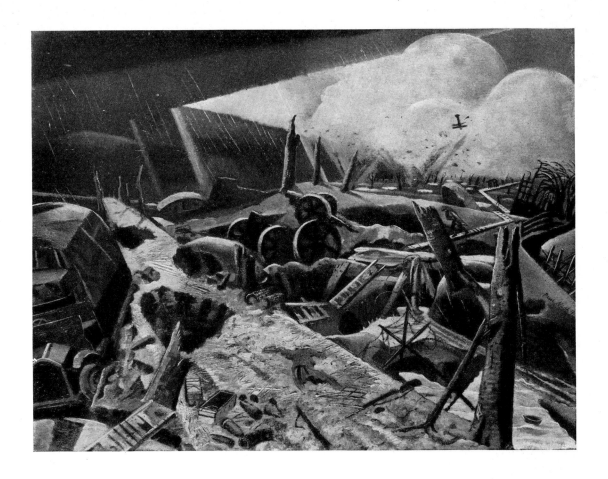

PAUL NASH. Void. 1918. Oil on canvas, 28 x 36 inches. Lent by the National Gallery of Canada, Ottawa.

A landscape of the Ypres salient.

Paul Nash was born in London in 1889. Painter, wood-engraver, poster and stage designer and illustrator. Studied at the Slade School. Early member of the London Group. Served in the last war as an official war artist. Has taught at the Royal College of Art. Ex-President of the Society of Industrial Artists. Has held many exhibitions in London. In 1933 founded Unit One, a group of abstract artists. Air Ministry Artist, 1940.

EDWARD ARDIZZONE. *Priest Begging for a Lift in Louvain, May 1940. Watercolor, 9½ x 12⅛ inches.*

Ardizzone was born at Haiphong, French Indo-China, in 1901. Studied at the Westminster and Central Schools of Art. Previously a gunner in the Territorial Army, he was drafted to serve as an official war artist when the present war broke out, and went with the British Army to Flanders. Ardizzone has held several one-man exhibitions in London and is widely known as painter and illustrator.

EDWARD ARDIZZONE. A Pub in Silvertown. 1940. Watercolor, 9 x 12⅝ inches.

A devastated corner in London's East End.

PAINTINGS AND DRAWINGS: THIS WAR

JOHN ARMSTRONG. *The Elms. 1940. Tempera on canvas, 20 x 27 inches.*

Even before the war this artist delighted to paint ruins. Here he portrays an effect of bombing.

Armstrong was born at Hastings in 1893. Studied at the St. John's Wood School of Art. Designed scenery for the Lyric Theatre, Hammersmith, and for Charles Laughton's films. Painted classical compositions in tempera about 1927, later turned to abstract art. Member of Unit One, a group of abstract painters.

EDWARD BAWDEN. *The Quay at Dunkerque. 1940. Watercolor, 12 x 19⅜ inches.*

Soldiers are seen entering an air raid shelter.

*   Bawden was born at Braintree, Essex, 1903. Studied at the Cambridge School of Art and at the Royal College of Art, where he later taught. Executed mural paintings at Morley College, London. Noted as water-colorist, book illustrator, and designer of wall- and pattern papers. Has executed posters for London Trans-port, and for Shell publicity in the famous "Shell-on-the-Road" series. Official war artist, British Army.*

MAJOR SIR MUIRHEAD BONE. Dawn—from the Signal Station, Dover, 1940. Chalk, wash and pen, 17⅝ x 29⅝ inches.

Ships bringing the last of the rearguard from Dunkerque coming around the South Foreland and entering the Gate at Dover in June, 1940. Painted on the site.

    Bone was born in 1876 in Glasgow. Studied at the Glasgow School of Art. Came to London in 1901. Member of the New English Art Club since 1902. Noted as draughtsman and etcher, especially of architectural subjects. Served as war artist in the last war; Admiralty Artist, 1940.

MAJOR SIR MUIRHEAD BONE. *The Exeter and Ajax Parade, 1940. Chalk, wash and pencil, 20¼ x 36¾ inches.*

The victory of the River Plate was celebrated by this review of the crews of the Exeter and the Ajax in the Horse Guards parade ground. At the table in the foreground are the King, Churchill and Chamberlain.

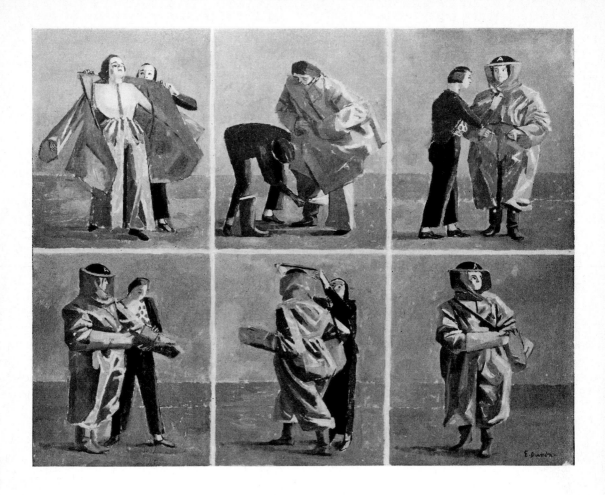

EVELYN DUNBAR. *Putting on Anti-Gas Clothes. 1940. Oil on canvas, 24 x 30 inches.*

Depicting the difficulties of getting into the special clothing worn by those exposed to mustard and other poisonous gases. This garment is so completely insulated that it can be worn only for a short time on emergency duty.

See photographs of gas masks, page 67.

PAINTINGS AND DRAWINGS: THIS WAR

BARNETT FREEDMAN. The Gun. 1940. Oil on canvas, 23¼ x 36 inches.

A 9.2-inch gun—one of many in readiness for the defense of the coast of Britain.

Freedman was born in London in 1901. Studied at St. Martin's School of Art and the Royal College of Art. Has staged and produced plays. Has illustrated several books with color lithographs. Designed the George V Jubilee postage stamp in 1935, as well as many posters and book jackets. Official war artist, 1940.

ANTHONY GROSS. *The Watcher. 1940. Gouache, 7¾ x 12¾ inches. Lent by Dr. Alexander Gross, New York.*

One of those who wait on London roofs to extinguish incendiary bombs.

    Gross was born in London in 1905. Studied at the Slade School, at Julian's and the Beaux-Arts in Paris, and for two years in Madrid.

KEITH HENDERSON. *Improvised Test of an Undercarriage. 1940. Oil on canvas, 30⅛ x 40 inches.*

A Lockheed General Reconnaissance plane is silhouetted against the open door of a hangar. This method of testing is contrary to all regulations but effective.

   Henderson was born in 1883. Studied at the Slade School and in Paris. Exhibits at the Royal Academy and is represented in important public collections. Author of Letters to Helen, *1917,* Palm Groves and Humming Birds, *1924,* Prehistoric Man, *1927. Air Ministry Artist, 1940.*

ERIC KENNINGTON. *Able Seaman Povey of H.M.S. Hardy. 1940. Pastel, 29½ x 21⅝ inches.*

Povey was one of the heroes of the First Battle of Narvik.

Kennington was born in 1888 at Chelsea. Served in France and was invalided home in 1915. In 1922 went to Arabia with Col. T. E. Lawrence. Also noted for his sculpture. One of the foremost portrait painters of this war.

JOHN MANSBRIDGE. An Air Gunner in a Turret—Sergeant G. Holmes, D.F.M. 1940. Oil on canvas, 30 x 25 inches.

Mansbridge was born in 1902.

RAYMOND McGRATH. *Beaufort Bombers. 1940. Watercolor on canvasboard, 14⅜ x 21½ inches.*
Wing sections awaiting assembly.

An Australian, McGrath is an architect by training and profession. At present he holds an important post
under the Eire Government in Dublin.

PAINTINGS AND DRAWINGS: THIS WAR

HENRY MOORE. *Pale Shelter Scene. Drawing.*

Londoners sleeping in shelters and in the Underground have provided the subject matter for a series of drawings by this artist.

Henry Moore was born in Castleford, Yorkshire, in 1898. He studied at the Leeds Art School, in London, France and Italy. Influenced by the art of primitive peoples, by Arp and Picasso. Member of the Axis group and the leading abstract sculptor in England.

PAUL NASH. Under the Cliff. 1940. Watercolor, 15⅛ x 22⅜ inches.

The tail of a Heinkel bomber (HE-111K).

For biographical note on the artist see page 15.

JOHN PIPER. (See opposite page.)

Piper was born in 1903 at Epsom, Surrey. Studied at the Royal College of Art. He has been an archeologist, musician (once a jazz pianist), journalist, one of the founders of Axis (a magazine of abstract art), and art commentator for television. After an abstract period in which he employed collage, he has recently turned to architectural subjects. Commissioned to make drawings of North Buckinghamshire under the Pilgrim Trust Scheme for Recording England. Member of the London Group. Official war artist, 1940, for A.R.P. subjects.

JOHN PIPER. *Passage to the Control Room at S.W. Regional Headquarters. 1940. Oil on canvas, 29¾ x 20 inches. For biographical note see opposite page.*

A corridor in one of the nerve centers of the British Air Raid Precautions System.

PAINTINGS AND DRAWINGS: THIS WAR

ROLAND VIVIAN PITCHFORTH. *Gravy Salt Factory, Birmingham.* 1940. Watercolor, 21½ x 29⅝ inches.

The effect of German high-explosive bombs on a factory.

Pitchforth was born at Wakefield, 1895. Studied first at Leeds School of Art. Served in the last war (as a result of which he is gun-deaf) and then continued his studies at the Royal College of Art. Member of the London Artists' Association and the London Group.

PAINTINGS AND DRAWINGS: THIS WAR

ERIC RAVILIOUS. *Norway, 1940. Watercolor, 18⅜ x 23 inches.*

Ravilious was born in London in 1903. Studied at the Royal College of Art. Executed mural paintings at Morley College, London, with Edward Bawden, and at the L.M.S. Hotel, Morecambe. Has illustrated many books. Member of the Society of Wood Engravers. Instructor of Design at the Royal College of Art. Official war artist (Admiralty), 1940.

PAINTINGS AND DRAWINGS: THIS WAR

ERIC RAVILIOUS. *Ship's Screw on Truck. 1940. Watercolor, 17⅜ x 21¾ inches.*

A ship's screw en route from factory to shipyard. During the winter of 1939-40 Britain was under snow for an unusually long time.

PAINTINGS AND DRAWINGS: THIS WAR

SIR WILLIAM ROTHENSTEIN. Air Chief Marshal Sir Charles F. A. Portal, C.B., D.S.O., M.C. 1940. Sanguine, 16 x 11½ inches.

Sir Charles Portal, former Commander-in-Chief of the Bomber Command, has been appointed Chief of the Air Staff at the Air Ministry, the senior executive Air Member of the Air Council.

SIR WILLIAM ROTHENSTEIN. A Sergeant Pilot of the Royal Air Force. 1939. Sanguine, 19 x 8⅞ inches.

Rothenstein was born at Bradford in 1872. Studied at the Slade School under Legros, then in Paris, where he knew Whistler and Degas. Member of the New English Art Club since 1894. Visited India in 1910. Served as official war artist to the British Army in France and on the Rhine, 1917-18. Principal of the Royal College of Art, 1920-35. Published Men and Memories, 1931-32. Knighted in 1931.

PAINTINGS AND DRAWINGS: THIS WAR

GRAHAM SUTHERLAND. Devastation 1940: Farmhouse in Wales. 1940. Gouache, 21¼ x 31½ inches.

For some time Sutherland has been hailed as one of the most gifted painters of his generation in England. While he is fond of abstract pattern, the solemn emotion and terror of war appear singularly in these new pictures.

Sutherland was born in London in 1903. He studied at Goldsmiths' College School of Art and later taught engraving at Chelsea Polytechnic. A member of the London Group. He has also designed posters.

GRAHAM SUTHERLAND. Devastation 1940: Solicitor's Office in Wales. 1940. Gouache, 31½ x 21¼ inches.

FELIKS TOPOLSKI. Scottish and Polish Soldiers at the Entrance to the Polish Camp. 1940. Line and wash drawing, 8⅞ x 11¾ inches.

Polish soldiers who had managed to get to Britain after the German advances through the Low Countries and France were re-formed and re-equipped at a camp in Scotland.

Topolski was born in Poland in 1907. Painter and caricaturist. He came to London in 1935 and is now an official artist to the Polish forces in Great Britain.

MIDSHIPMAN JOHN WORSLEY. *Part of a 6-inch Gun Crew in Action, the Shell Being Rammed Home.
1940. Wash drawing, 11⅛ x 14¼ inches.*

*Now only twenty years old, Worsley joined the Royal Naval Reserve at the beginning of the war, and during
the long hours at sea enthusiastically records the activities of his shipmates.*

PHOTOGRAPHS

The photographs reproduced in the section that follows are part of a large group selected in London by Mr. C. H. Gibbs-Smith and Mr. Misha Black. To them we have added a few by Miss Lee Miller, an American photographer resident in England.

They have been arranged in an impressive sequence of Civil Life, Activities of the Army and Navy, the R.A.F., and a group of significant forms of war-time objects, constructions and mechanisms. Perhaps in order to emphasize the collective and national character of all this pictorial evidence, the names of the individual photographers were not provided. Photography is, in fact, a somewhat anonymous medium. There are cameramen who are to all intents and purposes fine artists, but there are also cameras that have an eye of their own. But in the main its natural esthetic is documentary; it must usually be strained or tampered with to convey a private vision, and there is little or none of that here.

Although Americans have frequently surpassed the British in pictorial journalism, the esthetic and documentary effectiveness of these photographs is no less impressive than the work of the painters.

The present selection has been made on a basis of that odd or perhaps even accidental eloquence of mood that may be caught by the camera in bomb shelters, or at sea, or in the sky.

M.W.

DEPARTING SOLDIERS.

CAVALRY PATROL at dawn in the North of England. Constant watch for parachute troopers is maintained throughout the island.

PHOTOGRAPHS: ARMY

TANKS ON A COUNTRY ROAD. Once more, the contrast of tragic mechanism and the famous old-fashioned loveliness of Britain.

PHOTOGRAPHS: ARMY

THE MANUFACTURE AND RELINING OF LONG-RANGE GUNS.

TANK. A Christie-type cruiser tank, as used in the Libyan desert.

BIOMORPHIC FORMS. Barrage balloons being towed from hangars.

PHOTOGRAPHS: R.A.F.

REAR TURRET OF A WHITLEY BOMBER. At the top may be seen four Browning machine guns, with flash eliminators, capable of firing 4,800 shots a minute. In the center bullets may be seen above the ammunition boxes. The chutes on either side discharge empty cartridge cases. The gunner is in a highly vulnerable position. His is a night vigil, and often he must maintain his watch for ten hours at a time.

PHOTOGRAPHS: R.A.F.

R.A.F. GROUND CREW waiting for its planes to return. The return of a fighter plane is a grave and exciting moment. Damage inflicted by the enemy, though insufficient to prevent flying, may have crippled it so that it cannot land safely.

48

WHITLEY BOMBER. See page *47* for rear turret.

SUNDERLAND FLYING BOAT. This plane, of which the power-operated rear turret is shown, is as large as a Pan American Clipper and is used principally as a convoy protector. It has been known to shoot down four-engine enemy bombers carrying two cannon as well as machine guns. The workman is polishing a red, white and blue cockade which prevents its being mistaken for an enemy plane.

PHOTOGRAPHS: NAVY

BARRAGE BALLOON. To ward off Stukas, ships in convoy now also use barrage balloons. They must be shot down by enemy pursuit planes before dive bombers can be effective. The balloon in this photograph has been lowered; it usually floats at 10,000 feet.

PHOTOGRAPHS: NAVY

BATTLESHIP of the Nelson class, showing the nine 16-inch guns and, in the immediate foreground, the 4.7-inch gun used against high bombers. In the left foreground may be seen the ''pom-poms,'' which the British call a ''Chicago piano'' because of their appearance.

PHOTOGRAPHS: NAVY

SUICIDE SQUAD. *Ships in a mine-sweeping flotilla. The casualty rate in this service is said to be the highest of all.*

DESTROYER *steaming into action.*

CRUISER READY FOR LAUNCHING. The youth's gesture is typical of the quickening of popular pride in Britain's defense effort.

PHOTOGRAPHS: NAVY

NAVAL RESERVE SAILOR. This former fisherman, at the bow gun of a trawler, is setting the fuse on a twelve-pound anti-aircraft shell. The voice-pipes at his ears lead to the bridge.

PHOTOGRAPHS: NAVY

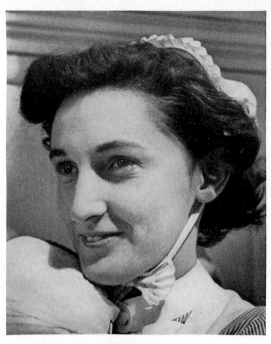

From the start of this war the virtuosity of news photographers has shown to all the world the unfamiliar beauty of the British race.

AUXILIARY FIREMAN; NURSE; FISHERMAN; R.A.F. FIGHTER PILOT.

PHOTOGRAPHS

SOLDIER; R.A.F. FIGHTER PILOT; WOMEN'S AUXILIARY AIR FORCE PILOT; SAILOR.

INTERIOR. Park Crescent, Regent Park.

PHOTOGRAPHS: CIVIL LIFE

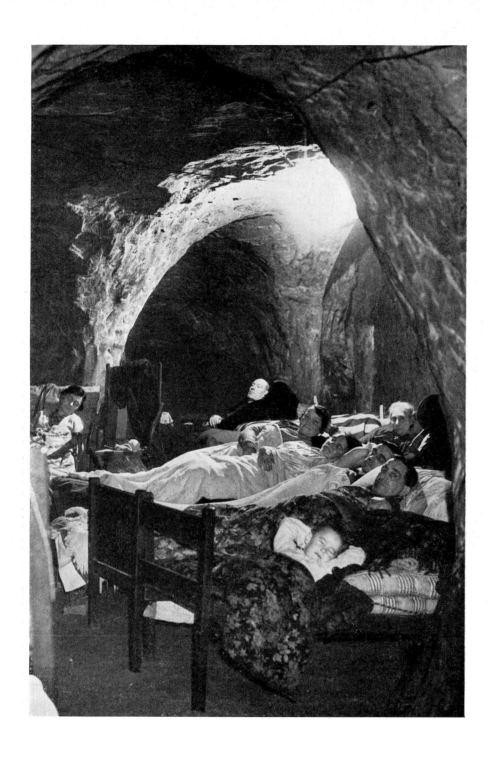

SOUTH COAST PREHISTORIC CAVE, near Dover, serving as a bomb shelter.

A HOP GARDEN IN KENT.

PHOTOGRAPHS: CIVIL LIFE

CONTRABAND. *Part of a consignment of rattan cane which fell into British hands.*

ST. JAMES' CHURCH, PICCADILLY.

THE HIGH ALTAR AT ST. PAUL'S.

MANNED BY WOMEN. *Many lawns have been plowed to provide additional nourishment.*

PHOTOGRAPHS: CIVIL LIFE

VEGETABLE-GARDENING in the moat of the Tower of London.

A BOMB-MADE PORTAL in the West End of London.

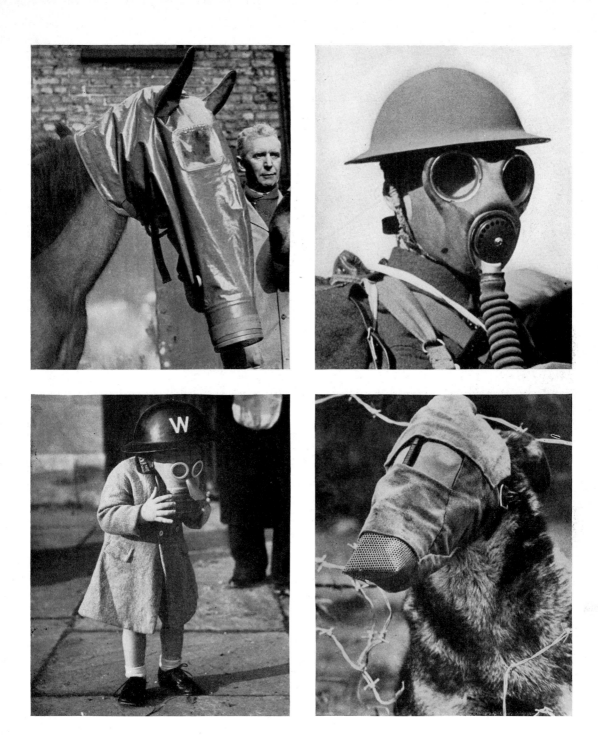

GAS MASKS. *Horse, man, child and dog ready for gas warfare.*

See photographs of anti-gas clothes, page 22.

HYDE PARK. Barbed wire and half-inflated barrage balloon amid familiar scenery in London.

PHOTOGRAPHS: CIVIL LIFE

THE NATIONAL GALLERY BY MOONLIGHT. Those who have seen London during the blackouts of this war all speak of the spectral beauty of its buildings by moonlight.

ST. PAUL'S. The night of the great fire, December 29-30, 1940.

DISASTER falling from the air grows more and more theatrical. Two heroines in a setting which Neher might have designed in Berlin in the twenties.

PHOTOGRAPHS: CIVIL LIFE

LONDON CHILDREN in an air raid shelter.

PHOTOGRAPHS: CIVIL LIFE

BURLINGTON ARCADE. A shopping center familiar to all American visitors to London.

ARCHITECTURAL RECONSTRUCTION AND WAR-TIME FORMS

It is a commonplace saying that omelettes cannot be made without breaking eggs—that one cannot create without some destruction. It is as true to say that civilized man cannot live among destruction without a desire to create.

In Britain now every bomb that falls is a stimulus to creation. No man, unless he is right down in spirit, can see his home crumble to dust before his eyes and his city made a ruin without dreaming of what that home or city may become when all this is over. That flash forward to a better future in the mind of the ordinary man is the point from which all planning and reconstruction starts.

For years there have been "planners" in Britain, far-sighted men and women who have talked and written and preached planning; and some of their talk has had effect. But whatever they have achieved here as yet has been won against the deadweight of the heaviest load of all—public indifference.

Now it is very different—a speaker or writer has only to mention "reconstruction" to excite response throughout the country from all those people, and that is all the people of Britain, whose physical need and ideals drive them to conceive this new New England which we must build on this side of the Atlantic. Planning has the headlines in Britain now in a way that we have never known before.

If all this is true, NOW, some may suggest, is surely the time for an exhibition of what planning means to Britain and what plans Britain has. If Britain is alive with ideas on reconstruction why can't they be shown both as a matter of pride and to encourage the others? Soon there will be much, but as yet there is nothing to show for our enthusiasms exactly because those enthusiasms are serious and have to be kept clear of meaningless utopianism. It would be magnificent if London could now, at this stage of the war, have a "plan" conjured from the brilliant mind of some new Christopher Wren, but it would be a magnificent distraction unless, which at this stage is almost certainly impossible, the plan could be conceived having inherent in it the means to its attainment. The plans we want must not be only the definition of an end, but must show the way to get there. This way can only be cleared by research, by education and the slow translation of enthusiasms into solid realization of the immensity and complexity of the problem. This is what we are up to in Britain now.

And so instead of plans for Britain and views of destruction and re-creation we show small symbols only of a sense of order. It is something in war time to have the machines of civil defense neatly designed. This neatness is a sign of order and of something clean and good which survives the inevitable disorder and mess of war. This is the folk art of 1941.

E. J. CARTER, B.A., A.R.I.B.A.
Librarian of the Royal Institute of British Architects.

MODERN BASTIONS. *Road blocks like these have been built on all strategic highways.*

GIANT CONDUITS *in fields to prevent the landing of enemy aircraft.*

BLOCKS *like these have sprung up at strategic positions on English highroads. The British call them "dragons' teeth."*

WAR-TIME FORMS

A.R.P. WARDEN'S POST.

CONVERTED TRUCKS. A standard design is used for converting trucks into ambulances.

HOODED LIGHT. One of these newly designed headlights must be carried by every vehicle during blackouts. Cars in government services are privileged to carry two.

CARTOONS

British cartooning, despite certain ups and downs, has been noteworthy for two centuries. The recent past has not been one of the high points; the greatness of Punch has diminished; Beerbohm and Belcher have done less, and nothing took their place. There is no Londoner to match our New Yorker.

But since the German enemy began to threaten, cartooning seems to have recovered the gusto of Hogarth and Cruikshank, and the violent intelligence of Rowlandson. The torch has been passed to a group of New Zealanders and Australians led by David Low, a merciless and combative idealist who will tolerate no timidity or delay of British statesmanship, while scorning but never underestimating Hitler and Mussolini. His polemical verve and grasp of current history reveal a literary as well as pictorial talent, and his cartoons have probably exerted greater influence upon the souls of the British people than any other art of this era.

But graphic oratory of this kind is not all the art of cartooning. It has always had, and still has, a legitimate aspect very near to mere entertainment. It can cheer and refresh and encourage mankind in its darker hours. This kind of humor is more important and valid now than ever, and for those who in time of war have scarcely an idle moment, it is often able to take the place of reading and theatregoing.

The cartoons which we show have been selected in London under the direction of Sir Kenneth Clark, save for a few provided by the Australian Newspapers Service in New York.

M. W.

WHERE NEXT, MEIN FÜHRER ?

DAVID LOW. "Where Next, Mein Führer?"

Low is the leading British cartoonist. He was born in New Zealand in 1891, has been cartoonist on important newspapers, and published several books. He is now political cartoonist to The Evening Standard, London.

" THE NEXT THING WE MUST DO
IS TO FAKE A REVOLT OF YOUR
BLACKSHIRT PATRIOTS AND PURGE
'EM OFF — LIKE RUMANIA "

HITALY

DAVID LOW. "Hitaly." From The Evening Standard, London.

DAVID LOW. "Hitler's Day." Cartoon from The Evening Standard, London.

GEORGE FINEY. "Doggo." February 15, 1941. Ink and crayon, 11½ x 18¼ inches. Lent by The Daily Telegraph, Sydney, Australia.

SAMUEL WELLS. "The New Order of the Boot—Germans Pouring into Italy." 10¼ x 14 inches. Lent by The Herald, Melbourne, Australia.

Wells served in the last war. Once cartoonist on the Manchester Daily Dispatch, he has returned to Australia.

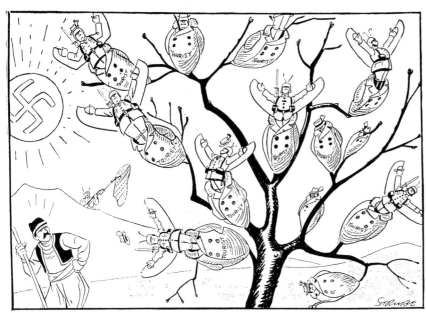

VERY EARLY SPRING IN THE BALKANS.

SYDNEY STRUBE, born in London in 1891, is cartoonist for The Daily Express.

HOW TO MAKE IT HARD FOR THE RAIDERS: THE SAFE WAY WITH DELAYED-ACTION BOMBS.

This "Safety first" method for coping with delayed-action bombs has been carefully thought-out by W. Heath Robinson. It is believed that the use of his device would eliminate practically all risk from the removal of those disagreeable souvenirs of Nazi visits.

DRAWN BY W. HEATH ROBINSON

WILLIAM HEATH ROBINSON. Cartoon from the London Sketch.

CARTOONS

"I suppose, Captain, they do keep these files up to date?"

"If I'd had my way, I'd never have let that fellow Tennyson give away all that highly confidential information about the Light Brigade."

"Hello, dear, it's Barnacle Billa speaking!"

"It may sound caddish, Sir George, but 'pon my word, I don't care if it is the breeding season."

CARTOONS FROM PUNCH.

POSTERS

The art of the poster is always linked to a particular problem of salesmanship or persuasion, and it is therefore especially subject to changes in popular taste and emotion. When it is weak, the weakness is usually due to old fashion, to time lag, or to a mistaken adherence to reputations, a confusion between celebrity and popularity.

When one looks at the posters of the last war, one is strongly reminded that the historical situation is not the same. The mood of the masses has shifted. The melancholy hatreds of Brangwyn and the fine illustrative conceptions of Pryse and others now seem inappropriate.

The shift in feeling of the common people today has necessitated a change in the style of appeal addressed to them. Government agencies, anxious not to run ahead of those they represent, often hang timidly behind or fall badly out of step. This is what happened in England at the beginning of the present war. This was the more regrettable because between the wars poster art in England developed extraordinarily. British work equalled the best done by the French and was superior to any done in the United States. The influence of abstract modern artists across the Channel, of the French designers—Cassandre, Carlu and Colin—and of the able American, E. McKnight Kauffer, resident in London, was felt, and British enterprise was quick to avail itself of their talents and of those of a number of its own fine modern painters.

It was unfortunate that the British Government did not use the talents of its own best men at the beginning of this war. It now appears that it has realized and acknowledged this anomaly and shortcoming; and more work as good as the present small selection may be expected to follow.

M. W.

"KEEP IT UNDER YOUR HAT!" Poster, 15 x 10 inches.

"BE LIKE DAD—KEEP MUM!" Child's poster by Reeves for the "hush hush" campaign. 40 x 25 inches.

"POST YOUR LETTERS BEFORE NOON." Poster by Lewitt and Him, two Polish artists now working in England. 29 x 36½ inches. One of a series issued by the General Post Office to inform the public of the emergency schedule due to war conditions. (Ordinarily letters posted at night would be delivered early the next morning.)

"SAVE FOR THE BRAVE!" Poster by A. Brener. 28¾ x 19 inches. Issued by the National Savings Committee. Lent by Bundles for Britain, Inc. Similar in its use of pictorial art to posters of the last war.

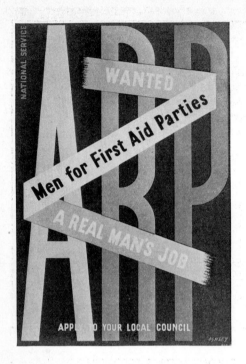

AIR RAID PRECAUTIONS POSTER by Ashley
Havinden. 15 x 10 inches. One of the first
posters used in this war.

"WE ARE VICTORIOUS — WINSTON
CHURCHILL, PRIME MINISTER OF GREAT
BRITAIN." Poster with Arabic inscription.
Montage, 28⅞ x 19⅜ inches. Lent by
Bundles for Britain, Inc. An example of the
adaptation of photography to poster needs.

"FORM A SAVINGS GROUP NOW!" Poster by
Pat Keely, 1940. 8 x 20 inches. Issued by the
National Savings Committee.

"IN A RAID—" One of a series of five posters
by Tom Purvis. 10 x 30 inches.

"DIG FOR VICTORY." Poster to promote home
production of crops. 28¾ x 18¾ inches.

THE ROLE OF THE ARTIST IN CAMOUFLAGE

Because we in the United States shall soon be seeing strange new examples of camouflage, we have undertaken to explain the several types of camouflage now in use by the British. Photographs showing the concealments of military and industrial objects are necessarily subject to censorship, so we have been strictly limited in the matter of illustration. This may seem a difficult or dull subject to the general public; but it should interest artists, and may suggest to them further steps in this military science which has always depended upon their sensibility and skill.

As yet camouflage is in its infancy; there are many ideas yet untried; and there is still a wide divergence between its practice and its potentialities, which are still to be fully appreciated.

The methods of camouflage are essentially the same in all countries, for they are as old as nature. Camouflage as we know it, however, arose from the last war—a logical answer to the introduction of a new weapon, the airplane. The immensely increased speed, range and size, both of pursuit planes and of bombers, have extended the theatre of modern war to include all vital points within their

A WELL-CAMOUFLAGED ARTILLERY POSITION showing the use of overhead nets garnished with strips of painted canvas. The disruptive design on the canvas covering and the gun barrel conceal the form of the gun.

range, thus making camouflage today incomparably more important than it has ever been before.

The role of the airplane in reconnaissance, photography and bombing depends upon visual PERCEPTION. Camouflage, through visual DECEPTION, has become a major means of combating its efficiency.

Total concealment or a convincing disguise is the ideal of the camoufleur. Where total concealment is impossible, as with ships, tanks and planes, camouflage can at least diminish visibility or distract attention from the true form of the object to such an extent that the bomber will overshoot the mark. Camouflage cannot protect a city from indiscriminate bombings calculated to shatter citizen morale, but it can successfully conceal vital military and industrial sites from enemy observation.

The practice of camouflage requires the collaboration of the military strategist, the architect and the artist. The military strategist decides what should be camouflaged. The architect and the artist possess, each in his field, the knowledge and technical ability required to meet the problems of camouflage design—they understand the fundamental relation-

AN ANTI-TANK GUN concealed with fishnet. The gunners are wearing white. A few strips of white cloth tied into the netting imitate the sparse pattern of snow on the ground.

ships of plastic and graphic representation through the use of color, form and texture. The training of the artist, his sensibility to color, his instinctive sense of form and space, fit him for the role of camoufleur. For although in painting he may portray the appearance of three-dimensional form and space on a flat surface, in camouflage he must strive for an opposite effect. He must reverse optical effects and use the technique of contrast to cause three-dimensional objects to appear flat. He must use the principles of design to dissemble the appearance of form rather than to delineate it. It is known, for example, that the brain comprehends simple and regular forms and areas of color more readily than complex ones. Therefore, in order to render a simple form more difficult to recognize, the thing to do is to superimpose another, more complex and contradictory. This is precisely what nature does in the adaptive coloration of its more vulnerable creatures and what man is now learning to do in camouflage.

Camouflage has frequently been prepared to simulate protective coloring as found in nature, and it is true that the most effective examples are those based on nature's self-preservation techniques in the universal struggle for existence.

Whether in the realm of interspecific warfare between animals or in the sphere of international warfare between men, the fundamental aims of camouflage fall into two distinct categories: MIMICRY and CONCEALMENT, and the various stages of the life of the butterfly provide us with analogies for both.

MIMICRY is the imitation of an altogether different object, which conceals the true identity or whereabouts of the animal or military objective. The cocoon stage of the butterfly's development illustrates the camouflage principle of mimicry. In shape, color and even texture, the cocoon resembles a curled dead leaf or a remnant of debris not calculated to attract the attention of the hungry bird.

BRITISH SOLDIER *weaving painted canvas strips into string net.*

The simplest method of disguising guns is to cover them with branches making them, like Malcolm's army in Macbeth, appear as a forest. City roofs are covered over with gray-green shavings to make them resemble grass, with only a few bright red roofs in view to simulate houses in the country. The anti-aircraft gun is hidden in a rude hut.

In addition to making the object to be protected look like something else, the camoufleur distracts the attention of the attacker by making something else look like the object. Parallel furrows plowed at the proper distance apart will look to the aviator like railroad tracks. A makeshift structure built where little damage can result, to imitate the contours of a military objective, will confuse the attacker with an alternative and cause him to waste ammunition. Dummy guns, airplanes and even villages are erected and carelessly camouflaged, to be discovered and draw fire from a more thoroughly camouflaged objective nearby.

The camoufleur must take into account the bold, subtle distinctions and variations of the color, tone

BRITISH CAMOUFLAGE, WINTER. Two Bren gunners.

and texture; the light, shade and cast shadow; and the surface area and outline which make objects distinguishable.

CONCEALMENT is accomplished through modifications in the color, form or texture of the object, according to the following four basic principles:

1 Color resemblance
2 Countershading
3 Disruptive design
4 Shadow elimination.

COLOR RESEMBLANCE

To use an example from another phase of the butterfly's existence, a green caterpillar is indistinguishable by its color from leaves and grass. The camoufleur paints night bombers with lamp black.

Battleships are painted a gray which blends into the seascape.

COUNTERSHADING

In addition, the caterpillar derives safety from countershading; its back, exposed to highlights, is darker green than its underside, which is normally in the shade. As a result it appears flat, even in the full glare of the sun. For the same reason, dark paint is applied to the tops of guns exposed to the glare, light paint to the undersides in shadow.

DISRUPTIVE DESIGN

The bold, subtle patterns of the butterfly's wing serve to distract the eye from the significant outlines which make the total shape recognizable. The

BRITISH CAMOUFLAGE, SUMMER. Field observer.

camouflage of the mass and outline of a factory or battleship serves the same psychological purpose of delaying recognition, a factor of extreme importance in aerial warfare, which is carried on at such heights and speeds that the delay of even a second is of great value in preserving military objectives. For if a bomber overshoots his mark and has to return to a second attack, the chances for the success of anti-aircraft and pursuit planes are greatly increased.

Disruptive design, or "dazzle" painting, was used in the last war with disastrous consequences in some cases. This was the result of the use of purposeless lines which in no way simulated nature. "Dazzle" painting, if properly handled, can nevertheless be effective in its end. Many changes have had to be made in the technique employed in the last war. The camoufleur, with a frightening twenty-year record of lethargy in his field, is forced to make discoveries and improvements at a rapid pace in order to combat the results of a tremendous and steady development in aerial warfare over these years.

SHADOW ELIMINATION

The butterfly skillfully and frequently shifts its position, tilting its body according to the angle of the sun's rays, in order to eliminate betraying shadows. This principle may be applied to some extent in the concealment of guns by shifting them to the angle giving the smallest shadow. But shadow is, in general, the camoufleur's most serious problem. Despite

CAMOUFLAGED SUIT to be used against a background of bombed buildings.

success in color resemblance and disruptive design, the shadow of an object may be identifiable at a greater distance than the object itself. This problem is somewhat relieved by the English climate. In new construction, shadows can be virtually eliminated by the architectural design of roofs which slope down to within a few feet of the ground, thus casting little shade. On existing buildings it is possible to break the solid shadow, so revealing to the aviator, by constructing irregular forms on the top edges of the building to break its sharp outline shadow.

Total concealment may sometimes be attained by the smoke screen, effective in both naval warfare and civilian defense. Entire cities can be hidden by smoke released from points selected to take advantage of prevailing winds.

By the methods enumerated above, the camoufleur can give the greatest measure of protection to objectives which must be recognized visually— legitimate military objectives such as men, guns, tanks, troop concentrations, matériel, munition dumps and factories. He cannot guarantee the immunity of anything, but any gains toward invulnerability are obviously justified economically, strategically and humanely.

CARLOS DYER

CATALOG OF PAINTINGS AND DRAWINGS

*Asterisk indicates that the picture is illustrated.

†Dagger indicates that the picture was still en route from England when catalog went to press.

Unless otherwise stated, items are lent by the Ministry of Information, London.

Due to exigencies of space not all the pictures listed have been hung in the exhibition.

LAST WAR:

GILMAN, Harold. 1878-1919.
Halifax Harbour, Sunset. 1918.
Oil on canvas, 77 ½ x 132 ½ inches.
Lent by the National Gallery of Canada.

JOHN, Augustus. Born 1878.
*A Canadian Soldier. 1917 (page 9).
Oil on canvas, 32 x 24 inches.
Lent by the National Gallery of Canada.

KENNINGTON, Eric. Born 1888.
*The Conquerors. 1920 (page 14).
Oil on canvas, 117 x 96 inches.
Lent by the National Gallery of Canada.

Mustard Gas.
Pastel, 24 ¼ x 18 ⅞ inches.
Lent by the National Gallery of Canada.

Colonel T. E. Lawrence.
Bronze, 16 inches high.
Lent by the Tate Gallery, London, through the courtesy of the British Pavilion, New York World's Fair.

LEWIS, Wyndham. Born 1884.
A Canadian Gunpit.
Oil on canvas, 120 x 142 inches.
Lent by the National Gallery of Canada.

MILNE, David B. Born 1882.
Seaford, South Camp from the Downs. 1919.
Watercolor, 13 ⅞ x 19 ⅞ inches.
Lent by the National Gallery of Canada.

The Belfry, Hotel de Ville, Arras. 1919.
Watercolor, 14 ⅛ x 19 ⅞ inches.
Lent by the National Gallery of Canada.

MUNNINGS, Alfred J. Born 1878.
Charge of Flowerdew's Squadron.
Oil on canvas, 20 x 24 inches.
Lent by the National Gallery of Canada.

NASH, Paul. Born 1889.
*Void. 1918 (page 15).
Oil on canvas, 28 x 36 inches.
Lent by the National Gallery of Canada.

Landscape, Year of Our Lord, 1917.
Mixed medium, 12 ⅞ x 17 ½ inches.
Lent by the National Gallery of Canada.

ORPEN, Sir William. 1878-1931.
Changing Billets, Picardy. 1917.
Oil on canvas, 35 ⅝ x 29 ½ inches.
Lent Anonymously.

*Man Thinking on the Butte de Warlencourt (page 11).
Oil on canvas, 35 ½ x 29 ⅜ inches.
Lent by Stephen C. Clark.

*Major-General Sir David Watson, K.C.B., C.M.G. 1918 (page 10).
Oil on canvas, 36 x 30 ⅛ inches.
Lent by the National Gallery of Canada.

ROBERTS, William. Born 1895.
The First German Gas Attack at Ypres.
Oil on canvas, 120 ½ x 144 ¾ inches.
Lent by the National Gallery of Canada.

ROTHENSTEIN, Sir William. Born 1872.
Houses at Peronne. 1918.
Mixed medium, 14 ½ x 20 ⅞ inches.
Lent by the National Gallery of Canada.

Ruined Houses at Chaulnes. 1918.
Mixed medium, 14 ⅜ x 20 ⅞ inches.
Lent by the National Gallery of Canada.

WADSWORTH, Edward. Born 1889.
*Dazzle Ships in Drydock at Liverpool. 1918 (page 13).
Oil on canvas, 120 x 96 inches.
Lent by the National Gallery of Canada.

THIS WAR:

ARDIZZONE, Edward. Born 1901.
Gunners of an Anti-Aircraft Regiment, August 1939. 1940.
Watercolor, 11 x 14 ⅛ inches.

Sleeping in a Shelter. 1940.
Watercolor, 10 x 14 ½ inches.

The Trek to the Shelters. Silvertown, September 1940.
Watercolor, 8 ¼ x 9 ⅛ inches.

Shelter Scene. 1940.
Wash drawing, 6 ⅞ x 8 ⅝ inches.

With the 300th—on the Move. 1940.
Watercolor, 11 ⅜ x 15 ½ inches.

Off to the Shelter. 1940.
Watercolor, 8 x 12 ⅛ inches.

With the 300th—Working Party in the Rain. 1940.
Watercolor, 8 ½ x 10 inches.

*Priest Begging for a Lift in Louvain, May 1940 (page 16).
Watercolor, 9 ½ x 12 ⅛ inches.

Louvain: Road to the Bridge, May 1940.
Watercolor, 12 ¾ x 8 ⅝ inches.

On the Road to Louvain, May 1940.
Watercolor, 14 ¾ x 22 ¼ inches.

The Bombing of G.H.Q., Boulogne, May 1940.
Watercolor, 14 ½ x 22 inches.

*A Pub in Silvertown. 1940 (page 17).
Watercolor, 9 x 12 ⅝ inches.

ARMSTRONG, John. Born 1893.
*The Elms. 1940 (page 18).
Tempera on canvas, 20 x 27 inches.

BAWDEN, Edward. Born 1903.
Halluin. 1940.
Watercolor, 17 ½ x 22 ½ inches.

*The Quay at Dunkerque. 1940 (page 19).
Watercolor, 12 x 19 ⅜ inches.

Carriers, M. T. Depot, Halluin. 1940.
Watercolor, 17 ½ x 22 ⅛ inches.

With the Quartermaster near Seclin. 1940.
Watercolor, 17 ¾ x 23 inches.

Factory at Armentières Burning after Being Bombed. 1940.
Watercolor, 12 x 19 ¼ inches.

BONE, Major Sir Muirhead. Born 1876.
The Deck Cabin of the *Campeador V.* 1940.
Pencil sketch, 6 ⅞ x 8 ⅞ inches.

*The Exeter and Ajax Parade, 1940 (page 21).
Wash drawing, 20 ¼ x 36 ¾ inches.

H.M.S. Victory in Wartime. 1940.
Wash drawing, 22 ⅛ x 30 ⅛ inches.

*Dawn—from the Signal Station, Dover, June 1940
(page 20).
Wash drawing, 17 ⅝ x 29 ⅝ inches.

COKE, Dorothy. Born 1897.
A.T.S. and Recruits Drilling. 1940.
Watercolor, 9 ⅞ x 15 ⅜ inches.

A.T.S. Air Raid Practice. 1940.
Watercolor, 9 ⅞ x 15 ⅝ inches.

CONOR, William.
Shipyard Workers Crossing the Queen's Bridge, Belfast.
1940.
Chalk drawing, 13 ½ x 18 ¼ inches.

The Evacuation of Children in Northern Ireland. 1940.
Chalk drawing, 13 ½ x 17 ⅞ inches.

CUNDALL, Charles E. Born 1880.
Return of H.M.S. Exeter. 1940.
Oil on canvas, 18 x 26 inches.

Tank Manufacture. 1940.
Oil on canvas, 19 x 30 inches.

DOBSON, Frank.
†Bristol, November 24th, 1940.

DUNBAR, Evelyn.
*Putting on Anti-Gas Clothes. 1940 (page 22).
Oil on canvas, 24 x 30 inches.

EURICH, Richard. Born 1903.
*The Withdrawal from Dunkerque. 1940 (frontispiece).
Oil on canvas, 30 ⅛ x 40 inches.

EVES, Reginald Grenville. Born 1876.
Brigadier H. Lumsden, D.S.O. 1940.
Oil on canvas, 19 ⅞ x 16 inches.

Lord Gort, V.C. 1940.
Oil on canvas, 20 x 16 inches.

FREEDMAN, Barnett. Born 1901.
*The Gun. 1940 (page 23).
Oil on canvas, 23 ¼ x 36 inches.

The Runway at Thelus During Construction by the 698 Co.
R.E. Air Component South. 1940.
Watercolor, 14 ⅜ x 21 ¾ inches.

GABAIN, Ethel. Born 1883.
The Evacuation of Children from Southend, Sunday 2nd
June, 1940.
Lithograph, 12 ⅞ x 20 ⅛ inches.

Evacuees in a Cottage at Cookham. 1940.
Lithograph, 13 ¾ x 12 ⅝ inches.

†Bombed Out, Bermondsey.

GROSS, Anthony. Born 1905.
Tank Practice on Training Ground. 1940.
Gouache, 13 ¾ x 21 ½ inches.

Sandbags in Bethnal Green. 1940.
Gouache, 12 ⅛ x 20 inches.

Medical Inspection of Recruits. 1940.
Gouache, 7 ¾ x 12 ⅝ inches.

Cleaning up after an "All Ranks" Dance. 1940.
Gouache, 7 ¾ x 12 ⅝ inches.

A.T.S. at Mess. 1940.
Gouache, 7 ¾ x 12 ¾ inches.

Recruits Waiting in Reception Room. 1940.
Gouache, 7 ⅞ x 12 ⅞ inches.

Rescue Party Clearing Up. 1940.
Gouache, 7 ¾ x 12 ¾ inches.
Lent by Alexander Gross.

Interior of Tunnel Shelter. 1940.
Gouache, 7 ⅞ x 12 ⅝ inches.
Lent by Alexander Gross.

Kensington Control Telephonists. 1940.
Gouache, 7 ⅞ x 12 ¾ inches.
Lent by Alexander Gross.

*The Watcher. 1940 (page 24).
Gouache, 7 ¾ x 12 ¾ inches.
Lent by Alexander Gross.

Barrage Balloon, 1940.
Gouache, 7 ⅞ x 12 ⅝ inches.
Lent by Alexander Gross.

Roof Spotters.
Gouache 7 ¾ x 12 ¾ inches.
Lent by Alexander Gross.

HARTRICK, A. S.
Seed Beds in King William's Garden, Hampton Court
Palace. 1940.
Watercolor, 8 ¾ x 11 inches.

HENDERSON, Keith. Born 1883.
*Improvised Test of an Undercarriage. 1940 (page 25).
Oil on canvas, 30 ⅛ x 40 inches.

KENNINGTON, Eric. Born 1888.
*Able Seaman Povey of H.M.S. Hardy. 1940 (page 26).
Pastel, 29 ½ x 21 ⅝ inches.

Leading Stoker C. Cloke of H.M.S. Exeter. 1940.
Pastel, 28 ⅝ x 20 ⅞ inches.

Leading Seaman Dove of H.M.S. Hardy. 1940.
Pastel, 31 x 20 ½ inches.

Squadron Leader W. E. G. Taylor. 1940.
Pastel, 26 ⅞ x 19 ¾ inches.

Group Captain Sweeney. 1940.
Pastel, 24 ¾ x 18 ⅝ inches.

†Group Captain B. E. Embry, D.S.O., A.F.C.

†Pilot Officer R. C. Dafforn, D.F.C.

†Sergeant F. W. Higginson, D.F.M.

†Sergeant J. H. Lacey, D.F.M.

MANSBRIDGE, John. Born 1902.
*An Air Gunner in a Turret—Sergeant G. Holmes, D.F.M.
1940 (page 27).
Oil on canvas, 30 x 25 inches.

McGRATH, Raymond.
  Assembling a Blenheim Main Plane. 1940.
  Watercolor, 14 ⅜ x 21 ½ inches.

  *Beaufort Bombers. 1940, (page 28).
  Watercolor on canvasboard, 14 ⅜ x 21 ½ inches.

  Wing Sections Awaiting Assembly, 1940.
  Watercolor on canvasboard, 21 ⅝ x 14 ⅝ inches.

MOORE, Henry. Born 1898.
*†Pale Shelter Scene (page 29).

  †Shadowy Shelter.

  †Brown Tube Shelter.

  †Woman Seated in the Underground.

MORLEY, Harry. Born 1883.
  †The Bombed *Toscalusa.*

MOZLEY, Charles.
  Kentish Lane, 1940.
  Watercolor, 11 x 14 ⅝ inches.

NASH, Paul. Born 1889.
  Flying against Germany. 1940.
  Oil on canvas, 28 ⅛ x 36 inches.

  The Raider on the Shore. 1940.
  Watercolor, 15 ⅛ x 22 ⅜ inches.

  Bomber in the Wood. 1940.
  Watercolor, 15 ⅛ x 22 ¼ inches.

  *Under the Cliff. 1940 (page 30).
  Watercolor, 15 ⅛ x 22 ⅜ inches.

  Down in the Channel. 1940.
  Watercolor, 15 ¼ x 22 ⅜ inches.

  Whitleys at Play. 1940.
  Watercolor, 15 ⅜ x 22 ⅝ inches.

  Wellington Bomber Drawn on the Day Hitler Invaded
    Belgium. 1940.
  Watercolor, 11 x 15 inches.

  Hampden Bomber. 1940.
  Watercolor, 11 x 15 ½ inches.

PIPER, John. Born 1903.
  *Passage to the Control Room at S. W. Regional Head-
    quarters. 1940 (page 31).
  Oil on canvas, 29 ¾ x 20 inches.

  †Coventry Cathedral, November 15th, 1940.

PITCHFORTH, Roland Vivian. Born 1895.
  A.R.P. Practice. 1940.
  Watercolor, 29 ½ x 21 ½ inches.

  A.F.S. Men at Practice with Trailer Pump, on the Banks of the
    Serpentine. 1940.
  Watercolor, 21 ½ x 29 ¼ inches.

  *Gravy Salt Factory, Birmingham. 1940 (page 32).
  Watercolor, 21 ½ x 29 ⅝ inches.

  Water Tank, Birmingham. 1940.
  Watercolor, 21 ⅝ x 29 ⅝ inches.

  Two Sheffield Steel Workers. 1940.
  Watercolor, 21 ⅜ x 29 ⅜ inches.

  Casting an Ingot. 1940.
  Watercolor and chalk, 23 ⅝ x 15 ⅝ inches.

RAVILIOUS, Eric. Born 1903.
  Passing the Bell Rock. 1940.
  Watercolor, 17 ¾ x 22 ½ inches.

  *Norway, 1940 (page 33).
  Watercolor, 18 ⅜ x 23 inches.

Ark Royal in Action—No. 1. 1940.
  Watercolor, 16 ¾ x 22 ¾ inches.

  *Ship's Screw on Truck. 1940 (page 34).
  Watercolor, 17 ⅜ x 21 ¾ inches.

ROTHENSTEIN, Sir William. Born 1872.
  *A Sergeant Pilot of the Royal Air Force. 1939 (page 35).
  Sanguine, 19 x 8 ⅞ inches.

  An Officer Pilot of the Royal Air Force. 1940.
  Sanguine, 19 ¾ x 7 ⅞ inches.

  *Air Chief Marshal Sir Charles F. A. Portal, C.B., D.S.O., M.C.
    1940 (page 35).
  Sanguine, 16 x 11 ½ inches.

ROWNTREE, Kenneth.
  Foreign Service Men in Hyde Park—Early Summer 1940.
  Oil on canvas, 18 x 30 inches.

STONOR, Jessica. Born 1913.
  Raiders overhead.
  Charcoal, 11 ½ x 11 inches.
  Lent by the artist.

SUTHERLAND, Graham. Born 1903.
  Camouflaged Bombers. 1940.
  Gouache, 15 x 24 ¼ inches.

  Picketed Aircraft. 1940.
  Gouache, 15 x 24 ½ inches.

  Devastation 1940: Public House and Masonic Hall, Wales.
    1940.
  Gouache, 21 ¼ x 31 ½ inches.

  *Devastation 1940: Solicitor's Office in Wales. 1940
    (page 37).
  Gouache, 31 ¼ x 21 ¼ inches.

  *Devastation 1940: Farmhouse in Wales. 1940 (page 36).
  Gouache, 21 ¼ x 31 ½ inches.

  †City. Fallen Lift-Shaft.

TOPOLSKI, Feliks. Polish, born 1907.
  *Scottish and Polish Soldiers at the Entrance to the Polish
    Camp. 1940 (page 38).
  Line and wash, 8 ⅞ x 11 ¾ inches.

  Polish Camp in Scotland. 1940.
  Line and wash, 8 ⅝ x 11 ¾ inches.

  Polish Soldiers at Blackpool. 1940.
  Line and wash, 9 ⅛ x 15 ¾ inches.

  The Salvation Army in the East End. 1940.
  Watercolor, 11 ¼ x 15 ¾ inches.

  †Fire in Chiswick, October 1940.

WORSLEY, Midshipman John. Born 1920.
  Lieutenant Commander R. Daintree, R.N., Gunnery
    Lieutenant, Resting before Dinner. 1940.
  Pencil drawing, 10 x 12 ⅞ inches.

  *Part of a 6-in. Gun Crew in Action, the Shell Being Rammed
    Home. 1940 (page 39).
  Wash drawing, 11 ⅛ x 14 ¼ inches.

  Five Members of a Gun's Crew on Watch. 1940.
  Wash drawing, 11 x 12 ⅞ inches.

  Group of Figures in a Sailing Boat in the North Sea in War
    Time. 1940.
  Wash drawing, 10 ¼ x 10 ¼ inches.

  Smoke on the Horizon. 1940.
  Wash drawing, 9 ½ x 12 ⅞ inches.

TEN THOUSAND COPIES OF THIS BOOK WERE PRINTED IN MAY 1941 FOR THE
TRUSTEES OF THE MUSEUM OF MODERN ART BY THE PLANTIN PRESS, NEW YORK